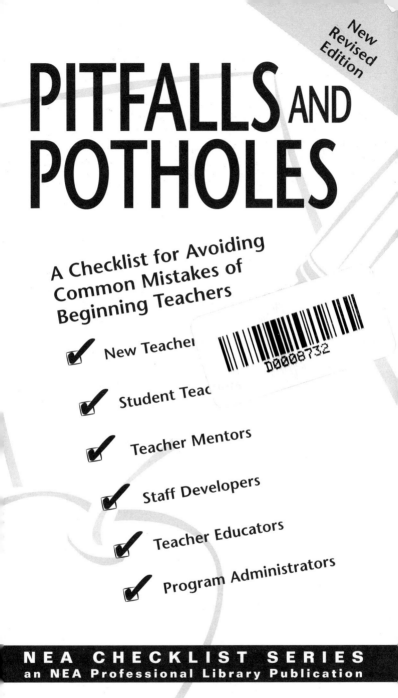

New Revised Edition

PITFALLS AND POTHOLES

A Checklist for Avoiding Common Mistakes of Beginning Teachers

- ✔ New Teacher
- ✔ Student Teac
- ✔ Teacher Mentors
- ✔ Staff Developers
- ✔ Teacher Educators
- ✔ Program Administrators

D0008732

NEA CHECKLIST SERIES
an NEA Professional Library Publication

Barbara A. Murray
Kenneth T. Murray

Printing History
First Printing: June 1997
Second Printing: November 1997
Third Printing: June 1999
Fourth Printing: June 2000
Fifth Printing: May 2002

Note:
The opinions expressed in this publication should not be con-
strued as representing the policy or position of the National
Education Association. Materials published by the NEA
Professional Library are intended to be discussion docu-
ments for educators who are concerned with specialized
interests of the profession.

Library of Congress Cataloging-in-Publication Data:
Murray, Barbara A.

   Pitfalls and potholes: a checklist for avoiding common
mistakes of beginning teachers / by Barbara A. Murray and
Kenneth T. Murray.

      p.   cm.   — (NEA checklist series)
   Includes bibliographical references.
   ISBN 0-8106-2151-7 (pbk.)
   1. First-year teachers—United States. 2. Teachers—
Selection and appointment—United States. 3.
Classroom management—United States. 4. Teacher–stu-
dent
relationships—United States. 5. Teacher orientation—
United States. I. Murray, Kenneth T. II. Title. III Series.
LB2844.1.N4M87 1997
371.102—dc21   97-38927
                                                   CIP

CONTENTS

INTRODUCTION

The nation's workforce of beginning teachers is changing. New teachers are coming to the profession with higher levels of maturity and more varied life experiences. Many of these teachers also leave the education field for other professions because of job dissatisfaction growing out of concerns about a range of issues, from managing student conduct, to balancing school and home life, to dealing with legal issues.

Not only is this attrition a serious loss of good teaching talent, but it is also a waste of the time and resources that went into readying those ex-teachers for the classroom. On the other hand, many of the pitfalls encountered by beginning teachers could be avoided if new teachers were simply forewarned, so they would know what to look for. This publication is intended to be that forewarning. It is also a road map around many of the potholes that beginning teachers can encounter on the road to success.

HOW SCHOOL DISTRICTS ARE ORGANIZED

One question frequently asked by beginning teachers is: "Who determines the rules and procedures concerning my job?"

School districts are governed by local school boards generally comprised of five to seven members. The local school board has the statutory authority to enact policies that regulate the local schools as long as the policies do not conflict with state or federal law. The chief executive officer of each school district is usually given the title "superintendent of schools." The superintendent is responsible for the overall daily operations of the school district. The superintendent also recommends policies to the school board, enforces such policies, and advises the school board when major issues arise. The effective school district superintendent delegates the authority to oversee each school's operations to a building-level principal.

The school principal is responsible for the daily operations at the assigned school. The principal's responsibilities include, but are not limited to, evaluating instructional personnel, enforcing school-district rules and procedures, and overseeing instructional and student-related activities.

OUR SURVEY SAID

To find out what public school administrators see as the common difficulties experienced by beginning teachers, we surveyed 60 administrators. The problems they identified can be regarded as pivotal factors that influence whether or not teachers choose to remain within the teaching profession. Pivotal Performance Factors (PPF) are factors teachers say cause job dissatisfaction. They also refer to teacher behaviors observed by the school principal that can affect the teacher's evaluation and may even influence whether the teacher continues to teach at that school.

We solicited school administrators' responses on a survey instrument with open-ended questions, and then we collected and categorized their responses. Although most of the administrators' responses focused on teacher behavior related to management of student conduct, this publication goes well beyond those concerns. To create the following checklists, we used not only the administrators' responses, but also our dialogue with beginning teachers and staff developers and our own experiences as teachers and administrators. We hope this compendium of strategies that have proven helpful to other beginning teachers in avoiding common pitfalls will help smooth the way for new teachers to continue and to prosper within the profession.

ORGANIZATION OF THIS BOOK

While this book is compact, it effectively addresses many issues important to beginning teachers. The following section descriptions should help lead you quickly to the information that is most relevant to your current needs.

• **Becoming a Professional** offers the guidance you need if you are new to the teaching profession. This section includes tips on applying for a job, preparing your résumé and cover letters, and readying yourself for interviews. It goes on to explain your role as a professional in the school where you are hired to teach.

• **Teaching with Confidence** explains how to best manage your students' conduct; how to effectively communicate with parents, students, and colleagues; and how to prepare lessons and facilitate learning.

• **Beyond the Classroom** discusses your responsibilities outside of the classroom, with tips on how to maintain a balance between home and school life. This section also includes important information on pertinent legal issues.

• **Strategies for Success** offers procedures for maintaining long-term success in teaching, including how to avoid burnout and where to go for professional growth opportunities.

• **Resources** contains a list of multimedia resources—books, videos, online articles and magazines, and annotated Web sites on related topics.

A Note to Beginning Teachers

Remember that teaching is a profession. It requires a commitment toward performing at a level beyond minimal requirements. To be a true professional, you have to show a genuine interest in lifelong learning and personal growth. You must continue to learn and grow in order to become a highly accomplished teacher. If you stick with your chosen profession and become a mature professional, you will find, that no matter what your age, your primary concern will be for the welfare and achievement of your students and their individual accomplishments.

You should recognize that before you can attain the confidence you desire, you need to become knowledgeable about all aspects of your school, such as classroom instruction, personnel services, school and district policies and procedures, students, and the community. You will find that both confidence and school savvy are necessary for surviving conflict and difficult times.

Even though you may feel you are being criticized in the media when you hear attacks on public education and educators, just remember—there is no other profession that so positively impacts society. Public educators like you have earned the respect that is bestowed upon them every school day when they are entrusted with parents' most prized possessions—their children. Such responsibility requires that you do your utmost to be highly skilled, caring, sincere, and dedicated.

APPLYING FOR A JOB

As a beginning teacher, you should take the application process seriously because you won't get a second chance to make a good first impression. When applying for a teaching position, don't fall into the trap of being timid. This is the time to trumpet your accomplishments and present yourself in the most favorable light. Here are five things to remember about completing the application:

❑ **1** Your completed application, application cover letter, and résumé are usually the school principal's first contact with you as a prospective employee. Handle the application process the way you would handle a work assignment.

- ▶ Plan ahead
- ▶ Be organized
- ▶ Be positive

❑ **2** Read carefully through the application before you begin to fill in the requested information. The application should be neatly typed—with no crossouts, whiteouts, or noticeable corrections. Be certain to complete all the items and supply all the information requested. Some employment applications may still ask for information that technically violates the law, but if you want to be hired, this is probably not the best time to display your legal knowledge.

❑ **3** Don't be modest. Be certain to include in the appropriate place any relevant work experience such as:

- ▶ Substitute teaching
- ▶ Volunteer work
- ▶ Summer jobs
- ▶ Work-study
- ▶ Work you accomplished as part of a team

☐ **4** Be aware that the principal is probably not interested in your pre-college activities unless they are extraordinary.

☐ **5** Normally, teaching applications ask if the applicant is willing to perform extracurricular sponsorships or coaching. Be certain to answer in the affirmative. If you have absolutely no activity experience or skills, do not say so unless specifically asked. Any teacher can be a successful assistant sponsor. Just follow the directions of the head sponsor. Don't worry, few principals will expect you to assume a head-coaching position. Plenty of other teachers usually want those tasks. The role of today's public school teacher often extends beyond the walls of the classroom. Don't be surprised to discover that schools sometimes hire teachers with coaching and other extracurricular sponsorships in mind.

> *NOTE: There are many different ways that school districts organize the application review, interview, and hiring process, for example, site-based hiring teams, central-office human resources recruitment, and charter-school application procedures. We use the terms "principal" throughout this section to represent the entity with hiring authority. Also, because much of the material in this section comes from our interviews with administrators, many of the tips are especially applicable to principal-as-hiring-authority situations.*

THE COVER LETTER

When you submit your application, it should be accompanied by a one-page cover letter. The cover letter should be neatly typed and must clearly indicate the position you are seeking. You can include some of your best qualifications in the letter, but don't exceed one page. Your application and résumé contain your complete qualifications, so try not to reiterate it all in the letter.

The following sample cover letter illustrates appropriate length (keep it concise!) and includes some highlights of the applicant's qualifications.

Sample Cover Letter

Don Barnes
1000 University Parkway
Deland, Indiana 99999

May 24, 20XX

Dr. James King, Principal
Royal High School
100 Palm Way
Kingston, IN 99999

Dear Dr. King:

This letter accompanies my application for the position of Band Director at Royal High School.

As a music education major graduating this month from the University of Central Indiana with a bachelor's degree, I am most interested in obtaining a high school position teaching instrumental music. I have maintained a 3.4 grade point average during my studies, have successfully passed all of the necessary state examinations, and I am eligible for Indiana teacher certification immediately upon graduation. Currently, I am completing my senior student teaching internship under the supervision of Mr. Walt Stratton at Lincoln High School in South Bend. In addition, I have worked for the past two summers as a counselor for the Lincoln High School summer band camp.

Enclosed are my completed application and resume. If I can provide you with any further information, please do not hesitate to contact me.

Thank you for your time and consideration. I hope to hear from you soon about an interview.

Sincerely,

Don Barnes

enclosures

THE RÉSUMÉ

Résumés are also important in your quest for a teaching job. Attach your résumé to the application, even if it repeats some of the information requested on the application form.

☐ **1** Your résumé is designed to show your accomplishments in the best light. Don't pass up this opportunity to shine.

☐ **2** Your résumé should be neatly formatted, easy to read, and completely accurate.

☐ **3** Put your name at the top along with your personal information, such as address, telephone number, and E-mail address, if you have one. Include references in your résumé, even if it means adding an extra page. The days of the one-page résumé are over. Principals now expect a list of references to be included with the application. Be sure to:

▶ Include complete addresses.

▶ Provide telephone numbers (very important).

▶ Avoid declaring that you will make "References available upon request." Applicants who do this make the job of the principal that much more difficult. With a large stack of teaching applications, the principal may just pass over yours and go on to another applicant who was thoughtful enough to include the references in the résumé.

▶ Include principals or assistant principals on your list of references, if you can. Typically, principals will call other principals or assistant principals to gain insight about candidates.

▶ Include the cooperating teacher you worked with during your student internship (another good reference).

- ▶ Try to include a member of the business community. Many school districts are interested in improving their relationships with the community.

- ▶ As a rule, do not include university faculty on your reference list. Unless the hiring principal has a personal or professional connection with a particular university faculty member, principals generally prefer not to rely heavily on references provided by them. University faculty tend to give positive references for their students, whether they deserve them or not.

Take a look at the sample résumé that follows.

JANE P. JONES
1000 University Parkway
Deland, Indiana 99999
404-555-1212 Home
404-555-1234 Work
jpjones@aol.com

Career Objective

To obtain a position as an educator in an innovative music department where I can use my experience as a band camp counselor.

Work Experience

1999–Present Music Library Attendant
University of Central Indiana, Clarksville, Indiana
Duties include supervising the practice rooms and checking out music recordings for study in the music library.

1998–1999 Band Camp Counselor
Lincoln High School, South Bend, Indiana
Duties included directing twenty high-school band students during the two-week band camp. In addition, I gave private music instruction and generally performed other assigned duties.

Education

2001: Bachelor of Arts Music Education, University of Indiana
1996: Graduate, Excaliber High School, South Bend, Indiana

References (included with permission)

Mr. Walt Anslinger, Band Director, Lincoln High School, South Bend, Indiana 99999, (404) 555-4321

Ms. Joan Ark, Assistant Principal, Lincoln High School, South Bend, Indiana 99999, (404) 555-4322

Dr. Susan Song, Professor of Music, University of Central Indiana, 1234 Composer Way, Clarksville, Indiana 99999, (404) 555-5689

THE INTERVIEW

If you are contacted for an interview, you must plan ahead and be prepared to present yourself in the best possible light. It is important to do your homework and learn about the school and district you will visit.

☐ **1** It is a good idea to call the school secretary, give your name, and say that you will be interviewing and would like to review any helpful information about the school. Such information might include student and faculty handbooks, a copy of the student yearbook, and the end-of-the-year school report published in the local newspaper. Volunteer to drop by and pick up the materials or read them at the school.

☐ **2** Remember that this is not the time to push to meet the principal. Unannounced visits can be perceived negatively. If the principal happens to pass through the office and the secretary introduces you, it is best to indicate that you are there only to pick up information about the school and that you look forward to meeting with him or her during an upcoming interview. If the principal offers a hand, shake it firmly. A wet dishtowel handshake may leave a negative impression.

☐ **3** Before the interview, you should anticipate some of the questions that the principal or other interviewers may ask. During the interview you must concentrate on your presence and demeanor. You should not expend all your concentration thinking up answers to questions that, with a little preparation, you could have had on the tip of your tongue. If you have developed a list of probable questions, prepared appropriate answers, and practiced your delivery, you will be free to concentrate on making a good impression.

*NOTE: See **Frequently Asked Interview Questions** for tips on questions to anticipate.*

❏ **4** Be on time. Arriving late suggests a lack of caring and professionalism.

❏ **5** Remember that the principal is sizing you up to determine whether you will be a team player. Whether you will fit in with the existing faculty is an important factor in the hiring decision.

❏ **6** Try to be yourself, but concentrate on maintaining a professional demeanor.

> ▶ Look the interviewer in the eye.
> ▶ Speak in well-thought-out sentences.
> ▶ Do not mumble, stumble around, or give long-winded answers.

If you aren't sure about how to answer a question, say something like "At this time I'm not sure—I would want to check with my colleagues."

❏ **7** If two or more interviewers are present, pay close attention when they are introduced. You should remember their names (take notes, if you need to) and address each by name.

❏ **8** At the end of the interview, you will be asked if you have any questions. This not only signals the end of the interview, but also provides you an opportunity to ask about the school. Stay away from salary issues. You can get salary information from the personnel office with one telephone call. Teachers are paid based on a negotiated salary schedule, with your specific salary being determined by your years of experience and your education. Try to ask an intelligent question, but if you come up blank, you might ask:

> ▶ "If hired, would I be working with a teacher's aide (or paraeducator)?"
> ▶ "What kind of clerical help is available for teachers?"
> ▶ About some other instructional support issue.
> ▶ About the school media center and its offerings (particularly in your discipline area).

☐ **9** Be certain to thank the interviewer for the interview. If there are multiple interviewers, call each by name and look them in the eye when you thank them. Don't bother to say something like "I could really be good if you just give me the chance." It doesn't help. Merely thank everyone, wish them a nice day, and leave gracefully. You will be contacted if a job offer is forthcoming.

☐ **10** Finally, make notes of the interview including any unanticipated questions you were asked. Remember, there will be other interviews.

FREQUENTLY ASKED INTERVIEW QUESTIONS

While it is impossible to anticipate all of the questions that you may be asked during your interview, you can be reasonably certain of some basic questions that will come up during a 30-to-60 minute interview. Six of the most frequently asked interview questions for new teacher applicants are:

☐ **1** Tell me (or us) a little about yourself.

> ▶ Don't take up the entire time with your childhood. The interviewer is merely trying to break the ice and get a feel for your recent past.
> ▶ Mention your parents, especially if they are educators.
> ▶ Figure on three to five minutes for this answer.

☐ **2** What made you decide to enter the field of education?

> ▶ Now is not the time to explain that you like having summers off. Hopefully, you want to

be a teacher because you like working with
children and find it rewarding.

▶ This is a good opportunity to include any
work or volunteer experience with children.

☐ **3** What do you want to be doing in five years?

▶ Generally speaking, any education-related
answer will do here. Do not indicate that you
only want this job until something better
comes along.

▶ Expressing a desire to enter into school
administration, counseling, school psychology,
or other type of school job later in your career
is fine.

▶ Principals like teachers who aspire to
improve their education; however, don't care-
lessly indicate that you want to begin your
graduate work immediately. Interviewers
might assume that you would be unwilling or
unable to sponsor extracurricular activities or
focus adequately on your first year of
teaching.

☐ **4** Would you be willing to sponsor a student club
or other extracurricular activity?

▶ If you say "no," then you are either ensuring
your future unemployment or indicating a
desire to keep your current job.

▶ Extracurricular sponsors are not quite as
needed at the elementary level as in the
upper grades, but all teacher applicants
should indicate that they look forward to
working with such groups. Besides, it is a
great way to get to know more of the
students.

☐ **5** How would you handle...?

▶ Typically the principal will give you a student
discipline scenario (usually one that has actu-
ally occurred in the school) and ask how you
would respond.

▶ Be careful not to underreact or overreact.

▶ Do not give the impression that you would respond to a child on the child's level. You should present yourself as a teacher who would take charge of the situation, remembering that your first priority is the safety and security of the children.

▶ Be certain to indicate specifically how you would handle the problem. For example, by having clearly stated rules and expectations and by learning to recognize potential problems before they escalate.

▶ Do not indicate your intent to rely upon the principal to solve the problem. Principals do not like teachers who use them as the first line of discipline. Teachers control their classrooms by having a variety of techniques at their command, which they can use with students who "act-out."

▶ Remember that most beginning teachers who lose their jobs do so because they are unable to successfully control their students.

☐ **6** What is your greatest strength? Greatest weakness?

▶ Be prepared to answer both questions, and don't balk at discussing your weaknesses.

▶ All persons have weaknesses, and hedging here will indicate a lack of self-awareness.

▶ Be prepared to indicate how you are trying to improve on your weaknesses.

☐ **7** There are many other possible questions that you should try to anticipate. You would be wise to prepare to answer a question about your philosophy of education. A simple response will probably suffice, such as: "I think the purpose of public education is to prepare children to become productive members of society while enabling them to realize their fullest potential."

UNDERSTANDING THE ROLES OF OTHER SCHOOL STAFF

Teachers having difficulties commonly complain about a lack of administrative support. Also, some administrators spend undue amounts of their time on menial tasks, community relations, or student discipline. When this happens, they often overlook their personnel development responsibilities. Just as there are many types of teachers, however, there are also many types of administrators and support staff. Your job is to get along well with the others in your building. To help you accomplish that task, here are some tips for better understanding the role of other school staff, including the principal.

☐ **1** Gather information that enables you to understand how the school principal, assistant administrators, deans, guidance personnel, bookkeeper, and secretarial support staff define their respective roles in supporting teacher performance.

- ▶ Review school staff job descriptions.
- ▶ Meet with the school principal about his or her expectations regarding your performance and the "chain of command" when requesting support.
- ▶ Meet with the assistant administrators and deans about their expectations as they relate to their specialized assigned duties.
- ▶ Meet with the administrator directly assigned as your supervisor to discuss specific supervision and evaluation criteria.
- ▶ Meet with the school guidance personnel to acquire information concerning student records. Talk with the counselors about what instructional support services are available for difficult students.
- ▶ Meet with the school bookkeeper and secretarial staff to find out about procedures for

handling money and obtaining and preparing instructional materials.

▶ Meet with your department chairperson or grade level coordinator and other colleagues to discuss their respective roles in supporting your needs. Again, you should inquire about the chain of command in the building for requesting help.

☐ **2** Avoid using the building administrator's office as the first line of classroom discipline. It should be the last resort. Here are some tips on how to increase your effectiveness by working with your colleagues.

▶ Ask for advice from the teacher or paraeducator who had difficult students last year.

▶ Ask your colleagues how they manage difficult students.

▶ Contact the parents of difficult students and ask what methods have worked in the past.

▶ Find out from colleagues and the school secretary which students' parents are the most challenging to deal with.

UNDERSTANDING YOUR ROLE AS A TEACHER

During the last two decades, a great deal of emphasis has been placed on effective teacher behavior. Research recognizes the importance of the individual teacher's reflection and self-evaluation.

☐ **1** The following effective behaviors frequently appear on teacher evaluation forms. Beginning teachers should regularly review this list.

▶ Room atmosphere sets the tone for the learning environment. Pay attention to color, space, and appropriate arrangement for multiple learning styles.

- ▶ Post important content (key points) on bulletin boards or walls. This is critical for some types of learners and demonstrates to administrators that you are stressing critical skills.
- ▶ Post goals/objectives for unit/month. Students need a road map of where they are going.
- ▶ Clearly communicate and regularly review classroom rules.
- ▶ Clearly communicate and regularly review expectations for student behavior and achievement.
- ▶ Post samples of quality work. Don't assume students know the degree of excellence you expect.
- ▶ Use formal and informal assessments of student skills and progress.
- ▶ Vary the instructional techniques you use to present information to students. Remember, not all students process information in the same way.
- ▶ Involve students in evaluating a unit when appropriate. Ask for feedback on how to improve the unit.
- ▶ Provide opportunities for students to reflect on their own learning. Journals are a great tool for this.
- ▶ Ask colleagues for feedback on lessons. Remember, you are learning as well as your students. Use video tapes to reflect on and improve your techniques.
- ▶ Demonstrate genuine interest in facilitating learning for all your students, both in academic and life skills.
- ▶ Be fair.

❏ **2** Effective teachers accept responsibility for initiating collegial relationships.

- ▶ Build collegial networks so that you may discuss course content and student performance outcomes with your peers.

- Review curriculum guides and materials used by colleagues.
- Visit classrooms of master teachers to explore other teaching techniques.
- Invite colleagues to observe your instruction and provide input to better enable your professional growth.
- Attend professional development activities.
- Attend faculty meetings.
- Become actively involved in collegial activities outside of your classroom, and share creative thoughts on matters such as curriculum development and school policies and procedures.

☐ **3** The professional teacher is expected to go beyond performing instructional activities and provide services as needed to students, parents, and the community.

- Communicate in writing. Send, for example, a detailed course syllabus or newsletter to every parent at the start of each school year or semester.
- Establish a time for a face-to-face parent–teacher conference whenever a student is performing below expectations.
- Establish a time for providing additional instruction for students who are having difficulties with assignments.
- Try to be aware of special circumstances that affect a student's well-being, for example, divorce, death in the family, or suspected abuse.
- Ideally, you should support community events that will enhance support for your classroom, the school, the district, and public education in general.

▶ Don't deliberately cause embarrassment for any student, parent, or colleague. Try not to embarrass yourself, the school, the district, or the teaching profession in general.

☐ **4** Historically, education within the United States has been regarded with a critical eye and supported by a thin wallet. The increases in student population and diversity require that the responsibilities of teachers extend beyond mere classroom teaching. Such responsibilities include, but are not limited to:

▶ Grade and attendance reporting.

▶ School-site strategic planning.

☐ **5** Teachers are expected to assume some duties in addition to their instructional responsibilities within the classroom. Find out what the norm is for your school. Failure to properly fulfill these duties can become a performance pitfall.

☐ **6** As a beginning teacher, you may disagree philosophically with the person who will evaluate your performance about which of your responsibilities are most important. The prudent beginner, however, listens to any suggestions made by the supervisor. By asking questions for clarity, you get a better understanding of what changes you are being asked to make.

IMPROVING YOUR PROFESSIONAL JUDGMENT

School administrators indicate that beginning teachers often show poor professional judgment. This is usually the result of a lack of experience and the tendency to focus only on their classroom rather than the entire school. The beginning teacher should be aware of how their decisions and behavior impact others within the school. The administrators we surveyed provided the following descriptions of what behaviors reflect sound professional judgment.

❑ **1** Arrive at work on time. Most collective bargaining (master contract) agreements contain language that specifies the minimum number of hours a teacher is to be in the school and on the job. If extra time is needed to allow for the preparation of course materials, or if the weather and traffic are likely to make you late, plan well ahead—leave home early and arrive at school early.

❑ **2** Leave the school building when it is appropriate to do so. Be aware that school procedure may require you to sign out through the office if you need to leave early.

> ▶ Leaving by way of a rear entrance and following the buses out of the parking lot typically is not recognized as appropriate.
> ▶ You should complete any urgent unfinished work, organize your classroom, and prepare your lessons for the next day prior to your departure. This practice not only saves you from being labeled as undedicated but also provides a relaxed, well-planned, and smooth start the next morning.

❑ **3** Attend meetings and arrive on time.

> ▶ Maintain a calendar to schedule your time.
> ▶ If you find that you have difficulty getting away from students who have after-class questions, allow extra time and graciously excuse yourself.

❑ **4** Show a positive professional attitude, especially with parents and community members. Off-hand remarks and inappropriate jokes, for example, "the three best things about my job are June, July, and August," can do a great disservice to the profession.

❑ **5** Maintain neat and accurate records, especially grade and attendance reports. Inaccurate grading has too often caused conflicts among students, parents, and the school. For example:

- ► Mistakes can affect whether high school students earn diplomas.
- ► Erroneous selection of valedictorian and salutatorian can occur.
- ► Even a mistake that gets corrected on a student's record can result in missed scholarship opportunities.

☐ **6** Even though taking attendance may seem like a bothersome duty, the gathering of this information is not only required by law, it can also help deter some of the undesirable behaviors associated with truancy. Furthermore:

- ► Always remember to have your grade book and attendance records with you during disaster drills such as fire, tornado, and bomb threats. Your attendance records can help school officials determine the location of each student.
- ► Secure your grade and attendance books when out of the classroom. Students have been known to tamper with grade books.

☐ **7** Realize that even though you are a beginning teacher and new to the field, your behavior has an impact on others within the school and the community.

☐ **8** Refrain from keeping students after class unless it is the last period during the day. Holding students late causes a great inconvenience to other teachers by delaying and even disrupting the start of their next class period. Lack of consideration by beginning teachers is often perceived by more experienced teachers as unprofessional.

☐ **9** Refrain from issuing passes to students to leave other classes, especially without permission from the other teacher. This type of request sends a signal that you feel the other class and teacher are not as important as your class.

❑ **10** You are responsible for the safety and control of the students in your charge. That's why you should develop a working knowledge of school law. See the **Beyond the Classroom** section for tips on how to avoid lawsuits.

❑ **11** Resist leaving students unsupervised (even for "just a minute").

❑ **12** Avoid placing a student in the hall outside the classroom as a disciplinary technique. Those students tend to wander and cause problems for colleagues and administrators. Check with others to see what alternatives school policy allows.

❑ **13** Resist the pressure you will get from students to allow them to ride home with other students without written permission from their parents.

❑ **14** Refrain from talking to students about other students or teachers. For that matter, refrain from talking to teachers about other teachers.

❑ **15** You should avoid even the appearance of impropriety. When in doubt, ask yourself the three questions below. If you answer "yes" to any of the following questions, you should give further thought and careful consideration before reaching a decision about what behavior would be appropriate. The discipline of asking yourself these questions and choosing the proper behavior will improve your professional relationships with other teachers, parents, and students.

> ▶ Will my behavior cause preferential treatment for a student, group of students, or program?
> ▶ Will my behavior violate my own expectations for how others should behave?
> ▶ Am I trying to avoid the consequences of my behavior?

While you are coming into this profession well-prepared to face many of the challenges teaching offers, there may be some gaps in your education. This section is devoted to helping you fill in some of those gaps by offering discipline strategies, tips on effective communication, and a brief look at some methods of instruction.

MANAGING STUDENT CONDUCT

Teachers and administrators agree that a major concern of all educators is managing student conduct. Our survey of administrators shows that the most troublesome behavior for beginning teachers is the confrontational student. Another common problem involves beginning teachers who allow themselves to get too close to students in an attempt to become a "buddy" rather than a teacher. Remember that the effective teachers manage student conduct with the force of their personalities. Focus on preventing student conduct problems so you can spend less time and effort remediating such problems. School principals suggest that beginning teachers should observe the following practices to ensure effective management of student conduct.

☐ **1** Recognize that you are always the adult, and refrain from getting too close to the students.

☐ **2** Teachers who teach younger students should exercise caution against too much touching. How much touching is too much? This is a gray area. Rely on instinct and common sense to govern your behavior.

☐ **3** When working with students on school-related projects such as musicals, drama productions, and athletic events, engage only in those social activities that are designed to build rapport and encourage the students. Prudently invite other professional adults such as assistant coaches, directors, and, perhaps, parent booster club members to provide additional support for you and the activity.

☐ **4** When disciplining a student, refrain from using physical force or threatening language that places you in a power struggle with the student.

☐ **5** Always maintain control and never lose your temper. Do not respond on the student's level of discourse. You will gain nothing by arguing with a student or becoming defensive when you are verbally attacked by a student.

☐ **6** Learn the building policies related to student conduct. You may be able to avoid many student conduct problems simply by being able to recite specific behavior expectations, along with the procedures for administering consequences.

☐ **7** Familiarize yourself with school policy regarding weapons, threats of physical violence, and school safety in general.

☐ **8** Resist the temptation to make threats that you do not have the authority to carry out. Most state laws, for example, limit the authority to suspend a student from school to the building principals and their designees.

☐ **9** Make a practice of speaking privately to individual students about inappropriate conduct. Do not "bait" the student, requiring him or her to save face in front of friends. This could result in a shouting match or worse.

☐ **10** Remember, if you expect to receive support from the administration and from the student's parents, your behavior must be supportable.

☐ **11** Make sure to keep the content of your lessons interesting to your students. Many discipline problems have their genesis in poorly designed courses that deliver content in ways that do not hold the interest of students.

☐ **12** Establish and regularly communicate classroom rules and procedures. Post and review them frequently with students.

☐ **13** Make sure your students know what academic performance and behavior expectations you have for them. Post examples.

☐ **14** Be consistent in giving feedback for student behavior and performance.

☐ **15** Manage the class by "walking around" and achieving proximity with as many students as possible, especially those students who are easily distracted.

☐ **16** Plan your activities to maintain instructional momentum. For example, take attendance while students are engaged in some seat work.

☐ **17** Learn to do more than one thing at a time. For example, begin orienting students to lesson topics while distributing materials.

EFFECTIVE COMMUNICATION PRACTICES

The principals we surveyed believed that beginning teachers often lack confidence and are reluctant to personally contact and communicate with parents. Never before has it been so important for schools to make good impressions upon their "customers." As a beginning teacher, you must also realize that in your harried day, sometimes the impression you make upon visitors is less positive than you might believe. Reticence can be interpreted by parents as bureaucratic arrogance, disinterest, or even a general lack of teacher competence. Schools cannot afford to squander community support for their policies and programs through inattention to the importance of effective communication practices.

The school reform movement has caused many states to legislate the establishment of advisory councils or other community input groups to improve school effectiveness and responsiveness to the community. Studies suggest that children who attend schools where teachers and other school staff practice open school/home communication often have more positive attitudes about schooling, which translate into greater student achievement, regular attendance, and lower dropout rates. Furthermore, involved parents are more likely to be active within and supportive of the schools, their programs, and policies.

Beginning teachers should make a point of developing and practicing the following effective communication techniques.

☐ **1** Establish a regular meeting time during the school day for communicating with parents concerning not only poor student behavior and academic performance but also positive behavior and increased achievement. It is always easier to first meet a parent under pleasurable circumstances.

☐ **2** Remember that words and phrases often mean different things to different people. Check to be sure you are communicating with clarity.

☐ **3** Recognize that two-way communication (each party speaking and listening in turn) is infinitely more effective than one-way communication. Avoid using educational jargon when speaking with parents.

☐ **4** Be sensitive to the customs and interpretations inherent to different cultures. If necessary, arrange for an interpreter for parents who don't speak English.

☐ **5** Develop an awareness concerning body language, and recognize that sometimes people send negative body language signals unintentionally.

☐ **6** Recognize sensitive areas of concern when communicating with parents, and anticipate parental reactions. No one likes to hear the insipid phrase, "It's against our policy." Parents do not care about school policy. They do care about their children.

☐ **7** Plan what you wish to communicate during a parent conference, and use vocabulary that is easily understood by the parents. Show examples to illustrate your point.

❏ **8** Familiarize yourself with the background of the student prior to the parent conference, and call the parent and student by name during the meeting. Ignorance concerning a child will translate to indifference by the educator and further serve to alienate the parent.

❏ **9** Resist pressure to know all the answers to correct student problems that may or may not be related to education. Don't be afraid to ask for suggestions from the parent, and encourage their involvement in solving problems.

❏ **10** Refrain from diagnosing conditions that require the expertise of a school psychologist or medical doctor. Such diagnoses not only lack credibility but are also unethical and likely to lead to a reprimand and additional expenditures by the school district.

❏ **11** Avoid being drawn into a defensive mode that will redirect the focus of the conference away from a student's progress and toward conflict with parents.

❏ **12** Pause and provide parents a reasonable time to vent their frustrations should the climate of a parent/teacher conference begin to erode.

- ▶ Make a point of not taking parents' concerns personally.
- ▶ Ask for clarification so you can understand why the parents are upset. Schedule a larger block of time for parents who are known to be "challenging."
- ▶ Maintain control of the conference by restating its purpose. For example, you might say: "I understand and share your frustration with William's progress. We are meeting today so that we can work together to establish a plan for helping William become more successful not only at school, but also at home."

☐ **13** Develop and practice a collection of successful communication strategies based upon scenarios provided by colleagues and literature. Refine your questioning skills. The art of questioning is critical to successful communication.

☐ **14** Invite a colleague to sit in as an observer during difficult conferences. The colleague will be able to provide feedback at a later time. (Give them things to watch for, for example, body language, wait time, or asking questions for clarity).

☐ **15** Refrain from making off-hand comments about the school, school programs, students, and school personnel. These comments will be repeated as "gospel" and could cause counterproductive and negative feelings throughout the school community.

☐ **16** Work to understand the communication techniques commonly used in school settings and the appropriateness of each. The techniques include face-to-face verbal and non-verbal telephone, written, and E-mail communications.

☐ **17** Work with colleagues to improve communication practices throughout the school to provide a more positive learning environment.

☐ **18** The following table offers words and phrases that can indicate either your friendliness and openness as a communicator or your hostility (even unintentional) and "closedness." Obviously, the effective communicator always strives to be friendly and open when communicating with parents or colleagues. Hostile statements often result in defensive behavior and unnecessary conflicts.

Friendly Words and Phrases	Hostile Words and Phrases
Will you....	Would you mind....
It works well when....	This is the worst....
We will....	Why don't you....
Can you tell me about....	It is not our policy....

How can I help....	I will try to....
What would you like to see happen....	I can't....
What can I do for you....	It is required....
[Your child] is capable of doing better with help....	[Your child] doesn't care....
I will do my best....	My classes are so large that I don't have time....
[Your child] could make better use of time....	[Your child] is lazy....

DELIVERY OF INSTRUCTION

Beginning teachers generally understand instructional methods, strategies, subject matter content, and planning practices. The school administrators we surveyed, however, cited the following common difficulties and offered suggestions for improvement.

☐ **1** Resist teaching strategies that are based only on the way you were taught when you were a child in school, and remember what you were taught in your college teacher preparation program. Vary your strategies based on content, learning styles of students, and grade level.

☐ **2** Recognize that you are inexperienced as a teacher. You may also lack varied life experiences. This inexperience frequently makes it more difficult for you as a beginning teacher to relate course content to real-life situations. You should seek out a variety of resources to help make course content "real" for your students.

☐ **3** Try to learn the characteristics of student differences such as culture, personality, gender, special needs, and learning styles. Use this information when planning course content, materials, activities, and instructional methods in general.

☐ **4** Familiarize yourself with the concept of "academic freedom." Generally, the local school board has the authority to determine the content of every course within a school district. Most school boards, however, depend on administrators and teachers to select and implement the material that should be taught within a given course. Because teachers work in a sensitive area of society, as individuals they typically enjoy little or no legal latitude concerning what will be taught to the students. Teachers in grades K–12, however, have some degree of academic freedom concerning their method of instruction as long as they have not been otherwise directed and if their chosen method is one that is generally recognized by their profession.

☐ **5** Understand that the U.S. constitutional requirement for separation of church and state requires that no part of the government, such as a public school, may promote or inhibit religion. So, no public school personnel should indicate actively or passively a time for prayer or "private meditation." However, students who wish to bow their heads, fold their hands, or otherwise pray silently, and who are not being disruptive, should be permitted to do so.

- ▶ Music teachers should be careful in their selection of music. Certain religious music, however, is traditional and proper for its academic value.

- ▶ Public school teachers in general should not display religious articles, photographs, paintings, or other forms of religious art unless there is a clearly defined academic purpose for such.

- ▶ No teacher should award extra points to students for attending religious activities.

- ▶ Teachers should honor any student's request to leave the public school during the day to attend religious instruction elsewhere. Such release should follow school policy and procedures and include the parent's permission and school principal's consent.

- ▶ Teachers are not permitted to penalize students for observing their respective religious holidays.

▶ In general, public schools should allow students wishing to distribute religious material during noninstructional time, and who are not being disruptive, to do so. The teacher should advise the principal of any such request.

☐ **6** The teacher should gather information about state and local laws and school policies concerning special subject content and activities such as sex education and animal dissection. Some states forbid the dissection of living mammalian animals or birds and define the procedures for use of nonliving animals.

☐ **7** When in doubt, the beginning teacher should discuss any subject content that may be controversial with the principal. It is wise to request written permission to use or teach from materials that may be questioned. The principal will probably respond to your request in writing and may include written policies and procedures pertaining to the subject. This written permission may come in handy for you in the future.

PRESENTING THE LESSON

The administrators in this study noted that because beginning teachers typically focus on their own performance in getting the lesson taught, they often forget to stay in tune with the students' reactions to the lesson. We offer the following tips on how to engage students in your learning activities.

☐ **1** Ensure that the classroom environment is inviting to all students and that no single group or type of child is unrecognized.

☐ **2** Invite each student to participate in class discussion, enabling each to develop interest in the lesson.

☐ **3** Monitor which parts of the lesson spark the most student interest, and focus additional questions and activities on those areas. Keep students on track.

☐ **4** Pause before the next lesson, while student interest is high, to give students time to expand and transfer their knowledge. Engage students in activities related to lifetime experiences.

☐ **5** Recognize that teacher-guided discovery methods tend to focus students on your objective while allowing them to take charge of their own learning process.

☐ **6** Resist discovery methods and individualized instruction that are so permissive that students lose direction, motivation, and the lesson's focus.

☐ **7** Do not lecture throughout the lesson. Students need to be active while learning.

☐ **8** Let students know that you expect them to master their skills.

☐ **9** Have students review a previously introduced skill while taking care of "housekeeping procedures," such as distributing and collecting papers or taking attendance. Try to cluster housekeeping activities together to maximize instructional time. By handling more than one housekeeping task at one time, you reduce your students' time away from the instructional task.

☐ **10** Recognize that different methods of teaching work better in some situations than in others. The following table shows different methods of instructional delivery and when each is appropriate or inappropriate. Use this table, advice from your experienced colleagues, and your own experience to determine which method might work best for you in any given situation.

INSTRUCTIONAL METHODS AND THEIR USES

METHOD	CHARACTERISTICS	EXAMPLE	WHEN TO USE	WHEN NOT TO USE
Direct Instruction	Provides basic facts that are necessary as a foundation for further learning.	Grammar rules, scientific laws and principles, music fundamentals (scales, etc.), fact-based instruction.	More effective with older students who have mature attention spans, when retention of facts is primary objective.	Less effective when students are passive learners (focus of lesson is on the teacher), younger students, or have shorter attention spans.
Inquiry	Helps students develop higher-level thinking skills.	Experimentation and research projects, field trips.	Effective with all students, and all ages, as active learners.	When instruction time is limited.
Individualized Instruction	Allows self-paced presentation of content by students.	Private music instruction, reading, math, etc.	When there is a significant range of abilities within the classroom.	When social interaction is desired or necessary, or when time constraints preclude.
Learning Centers	Encourages students to engage in self-paced discovery.	Geography, science, weather.	Effective with all students, and all ages, as active and cooperative learners. Most effective when teacher feedback is provided regularly.	When students lack necessary background and fundamentals, or if content is too elementary to retain students' interest.
Computer-Assisted Instruction	Provides students with a device for drill and practice, simulation, and solving computational problems.	Math, foreign language, stock market simulations, drafting, dissection simulations, vocabulary, spelling, etc.	Effective when drill and practice are necessary for memorization, to develop higher-level thinking skills through simulation, or when it is undesirable to dissect an animal.	When students have insufficient understanding of computer fundamentals or subject content.

This section will help you recognize important non-instructional issues and avoid the snares that can result from either ignoring these issues or taking on more than you should.

NON-INSTRUCTIONAL RESPONSIBILITIES

Because college and university teacher preparation programs typically do not emphasize non-instructional teacher responsibilities, beginning teachers often fail to recognize their importance. As a result, those administrators we surveyed provided the following suggestions.

❏ **1** Read the master collective bargaining agreement, and ask questions about those areas you do not understand. It is best to ask the principal, building union representative, or the union president.

❏ **2** Read your employment contract and school district and building teacher handbooks.

❏ **3** Be careful not to overextend yourself during your first year by taking on an overwhelming amount of additional duties and responsibilities.

❏ **4** Recognize, however, that it is your professional duty to assume a share of the noninstructional assignments.

❏ **5** Learn as early as possible the art of graciously declining extracurricular sponsorships when your family responsibilities or classroom effectiveness begin to suffer.

ORGANIZING YOUR LIFE

The administrators we surveyed reported that struggling beginning teachers often do not have control of their priorities and are, therefore, disorganized in carrying out their job responsibilities. They suggested the following practices.

❑ **1** Identify your responsibilities at home and at school, and develop a list of priorities. Strike a balance that makes you feel most comfortable to reduce stress.

❑ **2** Maintain a calendar to schedule school activities, meetings, and report deadlines. Include family activities so that they each will receive the appropriate amount of your attention.

❑ **3** Maintain files or folders that contain lists of "things I must do" and organize them by the day (prioritized), week, month, and perhaps year.

❑ **4** Always allow for extra time to reduce stress that results from the unexpected. Establish personal deadlines in advance of required deadlines, and set your watch and alarm clock ahead if that is what it takes to be on time.

LAWSUITS AND BEING SUED

Experienced teachers, beginning teachers, and teacher interns regularly ask questions about the law. Like it or not, the teaching profession is greatly affected by state and federal laws. The following suggestions are phrased as answers to the legal questions most frequently asked by school staff.

❑ 1 Can I be sued if someone is injured in my class?

Yes, for the most part:

> ▶ Although governmental immunity "once protected school districts from suit, this protection has been slowly eroded over time and school districts in many states can now be sued much like anyone else....The school district, however, is not the only potential defendant...teachers and principals can also be sued and held personally liable for injuries." 40 *Ed. Law Rep.* 1 (Sept. 3, 1987).

▶ A few states take a different approach and have laws that immunize teachers and teacher interns from personal liability for negligence committed on the job. Even these immunity laws do not provide a complete shield against being sued, however, because they offer no protection if the alleged wrong involves recklessness or if an intentional tort is alleged.

❑ 2 What is a tort?

Generally speaking, a tort is a civil wrong, or injury, to a person's body, property, or reputation. Torts can be intentional (someone intended to harm someone else) or unintentional (negligent). By far, the greatest amount of tort litigation concerning schools involves unintentional, or negligent, torts. For negligence to be shown, the following four elements must be present:

▶ The teacher owed a duty of some kind to the student;

▶ The teacher breached that duty by act or omission;

▶ The student suffered some physical, emotional, or financial damage, injury, or loss; and

▶ The breach of duty by the teacher was the proximate, or legal, cause of the loss, injury, or damage to the student.

❑ 3 What are my duties under the law?

Courts have held, depending on the factual situation of each case, that the following duties may exist in a school situation:

▶ Duty to supervise students.

▶ Duty to protect visitors.

▶ Duty to instruct students concerning proper safety procedures.

▶ Duty to equip students with proper safety equipment.

❑ 4 What is a breach of duty?

Breach of duty, the second element of negligence, is usually a question of fact.

▶ Whether a teacher has breached a duty is determined by the standard of "reasonable-ness." The "reasonable person" concept is considered an objective standard, i.e., in determining if a teacher breached a duty, courts will look to what a reasonable teacher would have done in the same situation. If the lawsuit concerns, for example, the actions of a high school physical education teacher, each side in the lawsuit will present witnesses, who are presumably reasonable high school physical education teachers, to testify about what a reasonable high school physical education teacher would have done in that particular situation. The defense, of course, will want to show that the defendant's actions were reasonable.

▶ To determine reasonableness, courts will also allow evidence of any school policies or guide-lines that may have been observed or violated by our hypothetical physical education teacher.

▶ Finally, the test of foreseeability is used to determine if a duty has been breached. Courts look to whether the accident or incident was foreseeable by a reasonable high school physical education teacher in the particular circumstance.

❑ 5 What else do I need to know to avoid a breach of duty?

The following list, while it is by no means exhaustive, can help you avoid some of the more common breaches of duty that can cause beginning teachers to stumble. In addition to complying with school and district policies and procedures, teachers must:

- Provide reasonable and adequate supervision.
- Deliver proper safety instruction prior to engaging students in an activity that poses a risk.
- Where appropriate, maintain facilities and equipment in safe condition and not only warn, but also protect, students from known hazards and foreseeable dangers.
- Report in writing to the school principal any facilities or equipment in need of repair that pose a threat to the safety of students.
- Report to the principal any incident where the teacher reasonably believes that a student has been threatened by another with serious physical harm.
- Report to the principal any suspected possession of weapons by students.
- Report any suspected instance of child abuse or neglect to the appropriate authority, whether the suspected abuse or neglect may be taking place at home, at school, or elsewhere.
- Be present at assigned duty stations such as restroom supervision, parking lot supervision, or hall supervision.
- Be familiar with emergency procedures dealing with fire drills, bomb scares, medical emergencies, or other dangerous situations.
- Be certain to maintain dangerous instruments, such as chemicals, tools, or athletic equipment, in a secure area.

❏ 6 What is meant by "damages"?

The third element of negligence is damages. Plaintiffs try to prove damages by showing injury or costs incurred. Defendants often attempt to cast doubt on the extent of the injury or dispute the costs incurred. If a student is physically injured in an accident, the damages may be determined by the medical expenses incurred plus other costs, such as a dollar amount that may be attributed to the student's pain and suffering.

❑ 7 What is "proximate cause"?

The fourth element necessary to prove negligence is proximate cause, sometimes called legal cause. This element is often difficult to prove and usually results in lots of discussion and argument in court. The usual method used to prove that a teacher's breach of duty was the proximate cause of an injury or loss to the plaintiff is to ask the question: "But for the breach of duty, would the student have suffered the loss or damage?" In other words, if a teacher had not breached his or her duty, would the damage or injury have occurred anyway? Could the teacher have prevented the loss or injury if he or she had not breached the established duty?

❑ 8 What must the plaintiff prove to win the lawsuit?

The plaintiff has the burden of proving all of the elements of negligence in court. If the plaintiff fails to prove any one of the elements, the defendant will prevail. The level of proof necessary in a civil proceeding is different from what is necessary in a criminal proceeding. If you watch legal dramas on television, you know that to convict a person of a crime, the evidence must prove the defendant guilty beyond a reasonable doubt. The "beyond a reasonable doubt" standard is a high level of proof. The level of proof necessary to win a civil suit is that of "a preponderance of evidence." This means that a plaintiff can prevail by merely showing that "it is more likely than not" that the plaintiff's version of the facts are accurate. This burden of proof is far easier to meet than what is necessary for a criminal conviction.

❑ 9 What defenses are available to protect me if I am sued?

There are three major defenses to negligent torts.

▶ Contributory negligence is probably the most frequently invoked defense. If the defendant teacher can prove that the student was negligent and therefore contributed to his or her own loss or injury—even if the teacher is also proven negligent—the laws of some states provide that the teacher and school must prevail in the litigation.

▶ Because the absolute defense of contributory negligence has caused undue hardship for some plaintiffs or unfair resolution of some disputes, many states adopted the law of comparative negligence, which apportions the loss or damages between or among the parties based upon their respective levels of fault or negligence.

▶ Another defense to a negligence action is assumption of risk. This defense basically asserts that the plaintiff freely entered into an unsafe situation with full knowledge of the unsafe conditions and risks involved. In a school environment, this defense has very limited usefulness. Courts recognize that students do not voluntarily enter into the ordinary education program.

▶ Typically the defense of assumption of risk is invoked when the lawsuit arises from participation in competitive athletics (for example, on the school football team). As anyone who has played football understands, the players forcefully contact each other, and it is quite possible for one or more to suffer injury even when proper safety precautions have been taken by the school authorities. Therefore, the players (with parents' consent) assume a certain amount of risk if they elect to participate in such contact sports. Students who play football do not assume the risk of negligence by the coaching staff, however.

☐ 10 Should I purchase liability insurance?

For most public school educators, this is a nonissue.

▶ The vast majority of education employees are protected against professional liability by insurance provided through the school district or coverage they get by virtue of their membership in the local education association or union.

▶ Intentional torts are generally considered to be outside the scope of employment, and in fact, it is not possible to obtain liability insurance to guard against liability arising from harming someone intentionally.

▶ A few states (for example, Florida) continue to provide some degree of governmental immunity to school districts and school employees.

▶ Prudent educators will contact an attorney or their local union representative to ascertain their rights, responsibilities, and legal status under the laws of the state in which they work.

[Adapted with permission from Survival Guide for the Florida Teacher, *published by IntraCoastal Publishing.]*

Planning ahead is essential for the first year of teaching. The most valuable time you have is the time between being hired and the opening day of school. New teachers should engage in extensive planning before school starts. Too many first-year teachers wait until the first inservice day to get started—only a few days before the doors open for students. These teachers are behind before they start. Catching up is difficult for a first-year teacher.

As a first step, count the days you have before reporting to the school. Fill out a schedule or calendar outlining your plan for preparation before school starts.

—From *The First Year Teacher: Teaching with Confidence (K–8),* by Bosch and Kersey (NEA Professional Library).

TEN PRACTICAL STRATEGIES FOR LONG-TERM SUCCESS IN TEACHING

The following are some practical strategies that have been developed and used successfully by teachers across the country. They are presented as a summary to this publication in the hopes of making good teachers even better.

☐ **1** Always remember that you are the adult professional, especially when dealing with students and parents. Even though you may be a novice in the field of teaching, your professional training should allow you to remain calm and resist being drawn into confrontations.

☐ **2** Refrain from making inappropriate statements likely to "bait" students, parents, or colleagues into defensive and angry behavior.

☐ **3** If a student confrontation is imminent, speak with the student privately, away from other students and teachers during an appropriate time that does not interfere with class time. If this is not possible or the situation is of a serious nature, request that a colleague or administrator assist you with establishing an appropriate time and place for the student conference, coverage of your classroom, and the involvement of appropriate adult support.

☐ **4** Make a commitment to speak with parents. Make every effort during the onset of the school year to become acquainted with parents by first communicating positive information to gain parental support. Remember that even though parents may not have formal training in education, they know their child better than you ever will. Tell parents that you value and invite their input for developing solutions to improve their child's school experience. Only rarely does a parent prove to be unsupportive following such a conversation.

☐ **5** Familiarize yourself with the teacher contract, master agreement, building procedures, and school district policies as well as laws related to your job.

☐ **6** Develop a professional demeanor that projects knowledgeability about the field of education and dedication to the overall growth of each of your students. You will be perceived more positively and given greater respect if you are knowledgeable about all aspects of the work you do. You can take charge of your own destiny by learning as much about your profession and school district as possible. Introduce yourself to others within the school, and ask questions when you do not understand something. Do not sit back and assume that others will volunteer help or even notice that you need assistance.

☐ **7** Maintain an appropriate level of privacy concerning your life outside the school, especially when you interact with students and parents.

☐ **8** Establish a balance between your professional life and your personal life so that stress does not jeopardize your mental and physical health and general well being.

☐ **9** Find out what resources and services are available to you as a member of your local, state, and national teacher's association.

☐ **10** Make an effort to understand the teacher evaluation prodedure in your school and district, including professional development requirements.

Well, there you have it—a compendium of strategies that should help you avoid many of the mistakes student interns and beginning teachers make. By practicing these preventative measures, you can reduce difficulties that prevent you from focusing on the part of your job that motivated you to enter the profession—helping children experience the joy of learning!

RESOURCES FROM THE NEA PROFESSIONAL LIBRARY

Best of Teacher-to-Teacher: The Ultimate Beginner's Guide. 120pp. 2000. (2917-8-00-C4)

Bright Ideas: A Pocket Mentor for Beginning Teachers. Mary Clement. 56pp. 1997. (2153-3-00-C4)

Building Parent Partnerships. Beth Christensen, et al. 96pp. 1996. (2911-9-00-C4)

Countdown to the First Day of School. Leo M. Schell and Paul R. Burden. 72pp. 2000. (2162-2-00-C4)

The Discipline Checklist: Advice from 60 Successful Elementary Teachers. Ken Kosier. 56pp. 1998. (2152-5-00-C4)

Innovative Discipline. Teacher-to-Teacher Series. 96pp. 2000. (2916-X-00-C4)

The Inspiring Teacher: New Beginnings for the 21st Century. Robert A. Sullo. 168pp. 1999. (2955-0-00-C4)

Let's Team Up: A Checklist for Paraeducators, Teachers, and Principals. Kent Gerlach. 64pp. 2001. (2163-0-00-C4)

Teaching and the Art of Successful Classroom Management: A How-to Guidebook for Teachers in Secondary Schools. Harvey Kraut. 128pp. 1997. (2004-9-00-C4)

The First-Year Teacher: Teaching with Confidence (K–8). Karen A. Bosch and Katharine C. Kersey. 168pp. 2000. (2014-6-00-C4)

Visit the NEA Professional Library's Web site at www.nea.org/books for information about professional development books and videos, or call 800/229-4200 to order a free catalog.

OTHER NEW TEACHER RESOURCES

Books

Canter, Lee. 2001. *First-Class Teacher: Success Strategies for New Teachers*. Seal Beach, Calif.: Lee Canter & Associates.

McConnell Fad, Kathleen and James E. Gilliam. 2000. *The New Teacher's Survival Guide: Stuff That Works*. Longmont, Colo.: Sopris West.

McDonald, Emma S. and Dyan M. Herschman. 2000. *Survival Kit for New Teachers*. Garland, Tex.: Inspiring Teachers Publishing Group.

Recruiting New Teachers. 1998. *Take This Job and Love It!: Making the Mid-Career Move to Teaching*. Belmont, Mass.: Recruiting New Teachers, Inc.

Shalaway, Linda. 1999. *Learning to Teach: Not Just for Beginners: A User-Friendly Handbook*. New York: Scholastic.

Skibinski, Chet. 1999. *Things You Didn't Learn in Ed Classes: A New Teacher's Success Handbook*. Beaverton, Ore.: High Ground Publications.

Teachers Network. 2001. *The New Teachers Handbook*, New York: The Teachers Network, Inc.

Torreano, Joanna Montagna. 2000. *500 Questions and Answers for New Teachers: A Survival Guide*. Norwood, Mass.: Christopher-Gordon.

U.S. Department of Education. 2000. *Survival Guide for New Teachers 2000*. *www.ed.gov/pubs/Survival guide/*

Williamson, Bonnie and Marilyn Pribus, and Kathy Hoff (eds.). 1998. *A First-Year Teacher's Guidebook: An Educational Recipe Book for Success*, 2nd edition. Sacramento, Calif.: Dynamic Teaching Co.

Wong, Harry and Rosemary Wong. 1998. *The First Days of School: How to Be an Effective Teacher*, 2nd edition. Mountain View, Calif.: Harry K. Wong Publications.

Online Magazines

Classroom Connect. Classroom Connects, Inc., Monthly magazine with classroom and curriculum ideas.
www.classroom.com

NEA Today. National Education Association. Member news, features, topical debates, innovations, and resources.
www.nea.org / neatoday

Teacher Magazine. Published by Education Week. Articles, book reviews, commentary.
www.edweek.org / tm /

Online Articles

"Advice for First-Year Teachers—From the 'Sophomores' Who Survived Last Year!" *Education World*, 2001.
www.education-world.com / a_curr / curr152.shtml.

"The First 180 Days: First-Year Teacher Diaries," *Education World*, 2000
www.education-world.com / a_curr / curr262.shtml

"The Secret's in the Little Things: Simple Tips for Successful Teachers," Linda Starr, *Education World*, 2001.
www.education-world.com / a_lesson / lesson134.shtml

"Who's the Mentor?" Alain Jehlen, *NEA Today*, March 2000.
www.nea.org / neatoday / 0003 / cover.html.

Videos

Partnership In Education: Helping New Teachers Succeed. Based on the pioneering work of the Santa Cruz New Teacher Project, this video promotes quality professional development for teachers. Includes classroom scenes and teacher interactions that show the challenges facing beginning teachers along with selected strategies of new teacher support and assessment.
www.newteachercenter.org

Teachers Network offers no-cost, streaming videos online showcasing the work of exemplary teachers, including *How Smart Are You?: Teaching to Multiple Intelligences,* and *Fishbowl: Using Action Research to Achieve Standards.*
www.teachersnetwork.org / media /

Teaching Teachers. Teacher TV Episode #41. 1995. An NEA Professional Library videotape that shows a professional development school in action. VHS video, 22 minutes. Item #7790-3-00-F, $15.95.

Web Sites

ABC Teach—Free printables for classroom and home use including theme units, report helpers, self-assessments, forms.
www.abcteach.org/

Classroom Connect—Learning resources for K–12 teachers and students.
www.classroom.com

The Creative Teacher Site—Promotes creative teaching and professional enthusiasm.
www.creativeteachingsite.com/

Education World—Sponsored by American Fidelity Educational Services, a partner of NEA, this site offers articles on new trends, lesson planning, university and school links, employment opportunities, message boards, and online mentoring.
www.educationworld.com/

Educational Resources Information Center (ERIC)—Federally funded, nationwide information network provided by the National Library of Education, U.S. Department of Education.
www.ericsp.org/

The Educators' Network—Tools and resources free of charge to teachers. The site also includes theme units, lesson plans, and worksheets.
www.theeducatorsnetwork.com/

Gateway to Educational Materials (GEM)— Sponsored by the U.S. Department of Education's National Library of Education, GEM is a search engine for the many Web sites that include teacher lesson plans and other classroom resources.
http://thegateway.org/

Inspiring Teachers—Beginning teacher's toolbox.
www.inspiringteachers.com/

Learning Network Teacher Channel—Lesson plans, teacher tools, classroom management, and professional development resources.
www.teachervision.com

The Learning Space—"For teachers, by teachers, and about teachers," site contains information about designing instruction, technology in the classroom, and professional development plans and programs.
www.learningspace.org/

MiddleWeb's The First Days of Middle School— Developed for new middle school teachers, this resource is packed full of advice and tips for *any* teacher, new or experienced!
www.middleweb.com/1stDResources.html

Mighty Mentors—Pairs new and student teachers with experienced teachers in mentoring partnerships, a free service provided by Teaching.com.
www.mightymentors.com

New Teacher Center—National resource dedicated to teacher development and the support of programs and practices that promote excellence and diversity in America's teaching force.
www.newteachercenter.org/

NewTeacher.Com—Non-commercial Web site serving as an advocate for new teachers.
www.newteacher.com/

Sites for Teachers—Links to teacher resources and educational sites ranked by popularity.
www.sitesforteachers.com/

TappedIn.org—Informal collaborative activities with colleagues
www.tappedin.org/

Teachers.net—Chatrooms, message boards, live meetings and conferences, and teacher mailrings.
www.teachers.net/

USC Clearinghouse of Resources for Beginning Teacher Support & Assessment—Collection of online resources for new teachers and those who support them.
www.usc.edu/dept/education/CMMR/CMMR_BTSA_home.html